Journey Through The Inside Of A Poet's Mind 2

Copyright © 2022 Wohali Amayi

Introduction

The Announcer: *Greetings Ladies and Gentlemen! Welcome 2 a special edition on WFYM! I am The Announcer and we have a great show 4 u here. I am honored 2 welcome back the poet who brought u his last year release "Journey Through The Inside Of A Poet's Mind." He is back with his sequel entitled "Journey Through The Inside Of A Poet's Mind 2." We will chat with him later in the show. And now, I want u 2 get comfortable, have a snack, a drink. Without further ado, allow me 2 welcome 2 the show, a great round of applause 4 Wohali Amayi!!*

The Journey Continues!

<u>Sunrise</u>

A light shinin' through my window
I raise my head from my pillow
The warm morning sun kisses my face
The warmth of the rays fills my place
A good night's rest
2 wake up feelin' refreshed is the best
A cup of orange juice
Time 2 get loose
Lookin' at the clear blue sky
As I watch a group of birds fly
A great day 2 walk and energize
In the sunrise.

<u>Energy</u>

It's in u and me
We all have energy
The energy of the sun gives u heat
The energy of love can be sweet
Gives u light
Big and bright
Energy in the air is soothin'
Energy in your body keeps u movin'
Energy puts a smile on our face
It travels through the outer space
Like a boomerang, it comes back
Keep it on track
Feel it spiritually
Feel the beautiful touch of energy.

<u>Smile</u>

Open your eyes 2 wake up 2 a new day
Smile
Go outside, get energized from the sun's ray
Smile
Hang with family and friends
Smile
Enjoy the weekends
Smile
Feel the love bug
Give someone a hug
Smile
Help anybody
Cheer up somebody
Take their frown
Turn it upside down
Make them smile
Everybody needs 2 smile
Feel happy, give it a chance
Feel the joy, do a little dance
Smile!

In The Snow With U

Outside my window
The ground covered with snow
Let's go outside 4 a while
Holdin' hands, lookin' at each other's smile
Make a snowman, big and tall
Havin' fights with a snowball
A row of angels in the snow
At night, we'll watch them glow
From the inside sippin' a sweet treat
Cuddlin' each other with our body heat
Watchin' the snow fall
We enjoyed ourselves, we had a ball.

Thankful

People should be grateful
Are u thankful?
Be thankful u woke up this morning
Be thankful 4 your eyes 2 see everything
Be thankful 4 your nose
2 smell a beautiful red rose
Listen 2 the sweet sounds u hear
Be thankful u have 2 ears
A mouth 2 talk
A pair of legs and feet 2 walk
Be thankful 4 the sun 2 give u energy
The air u breathe, the clear blue sky
The natural trees give u shade 2 keep cool
Be thankful 2 enjoy a day in a pool
Give thanks 4 the nutrients 2 live
Be thankful 4 the love u give
Be thankful 4 family surroundin' u
Be thankful 4 friends supportin' u
Be thankful 2 see the stars shinin' bright
Be thankful u sleep peacefully at night
Take a look in the mirror
Everything u see is crystal clear
Ask yourself
"Am I thankful?"

<u>Earth's Ground</u>

Sun warms earth's ground
Wind cools earth's ground
Rain moisturizes earth's ground
Snow covers earth's ground
Trees grow on earth's ground
Leaves fall on earth's ground
Seeds u plant, blossoms beautiful flowers
With the help of rain showers
Children play
Time flies away
The green grass, nice and neat
Feel it with your hands and your feet
Enjoy the earth's ground
Love the earth's ground.

A Bird's Point Of View

Chillin' under the shaded tree
All alone, being free
Watchin' the birds fly
Flyin' free in the sunny blue sky
Listenin' 2 them chirpin'
Wonderin' what they're sayin'
From their view, people are small
Up close, the people are tall
Glad we can fly far
Try not 2 get hit by a car
Up here, it's simple and plain
We look out 4 airplanes
Lookin' down at the tall trees
Thick and full with green leaves
Build a nest
Give me a place 2 rest
If I was a bird
I'll travel with them
I'll talk with them
Translate their chirps word 4 word.

Spread The Words

Sittin' alone on a beautiful day
Thinkin' of words 2 say
Lots of time 2 spare
Plenty 2 share
Watchin' the birds in the sky flyin'
My words are pebbles in the river floatin'
Messages sent with the fishes
O Mighty One, grant my wishes
Share my visions
Let them flow without collisions
Are u listenin' Minnesota?
Share it with Wisconsin and Iowa
Pass it 2 Illinois, Missouri and Kentucky
Send it 2 Tennessee, Arkansas and Mississippi
Give it 2 Louisiana, let it flow
Into the Gulf Of Mexico, my words glow
Thank u O Mighty One
My mission is accomplished and done.

Around The World Blues

I look around and see a lot 2 be blue about
I feel like standin' in one place and shout
WHY OH WHY!
Why the world have 2 cry?
2 many things happenin'
The world is crumblin'
It's not businesslike
Makin' gas and food prices spike
We got the war blues
We got the eyesore blues
Teenagers are mothers
30-year-olds are grandmothers
Babies makin' babies blues
Babies killin' babies blues
I can't get a job blues
I got beaten up by a mob blues
Stop makin' the world sad
Quit bein' mad
I got a big tummy blues
I have no money blues
I ran out of gas blues
I failed in my class blues
My car ran into a pole blues
My shoes have no sole blues
Somebody slapped me blues
I want 2 be free
My hair is nappy
So what, I'm happy
What's wrong with that?
It's funny though, I'll sport it without a hat
I guess without the blues
We can't fix the problems we deal with, that's true.

<u>One</u>

Let me grab my pen
I take a deep breath, count 2 ten
One mind
Got 2 unwind
Relax my soul
Achieve one goal
Give me one hour
From the garden, I pick one flower
Place it in one vase
A smile from one's face
One life 2 live
One love 2 give
One world turn
One fire 2 burn
I spend one dollar
I pop one collar
One light beam
Grant one wish from a dream
One choice
Listen 2 my one voice
No need 2 rehearse
Share it with one universe.

Life From A Seed

One givin' a seed
Only u can do a good deed
Plant the seed somewhere warm
Protect it from harm
Give it plenty of H2O
Nutrients 2 help it grow
Light 2 give it energy
Watch it bloom freely
Watch it grow tall, full and strong
Lots of love worth lifelong
Take a piece from life's creation
Spread it around 2 form a new generation.

Priceless

Gas by the gallon, two ninety-nine
Foods on the incline
Give me break, please
Payin' all these fees
Gotta have your wants and needs
Spend a dollar on sunflower seeds
Most of the world has a price tag
Even a brown paper bag
Can u put a price on happiness?
My smile is priceless
U can't buy my time
Keep your dime
No matter how much u collect
There's no price 4 my intellect
My love is priceless
My legacy is priceless
U can't even pay 4 this line (with M-O-N-E-Y)
It's all mine (don't even T-R-Y)
It's priceless.

Mixture Of Spices

Grab a skillet or a pot
Grab some ingredients 2 hit the spot
Steam some vegetables with water
Melt some butter
Salt, pepper, sugar
I smile like a professional cooker
Ooooooo yeah!
Add some rosemary and mint
Just a hint
Ginger, maybe some cinnamon
Sprinkle some nutmeg, a dash of cumin
Pep it up with some cayenne
Gotta spice it up every now and then
Oh yeah babe!
A kiss 2 the sky
As I wink my eye
Can't live without the spices!

Lookin' 4 A Friend

Searchin' 4 u high and low
I look 4 the glow
Will u be the one?
Will u be my friend?
Through thick and thin
Will u listen 2 me?
Would u laugh with me?
Would u hang with me 4 awhile?
Can I make u smile?
Can u keep me from doin' wrong?
Can u show me where I belong?
Will u pick me up when I fall?
Will u be there when I call?
Who doesn't fuss and fight?
Even if it's day or night?
There's a space 4 forgiveness
There's a space 4 love and happiness
I'll support u
U support me
Forever friendship, you'll see
Let's band together, u and me
Let it begin
I'll take u in.

Believe II

U got 2 see it
In order 2 believe it
That's what people say
That's right, true statement everyday
Believe it, u woke up
Sip coffee from your cup
Mother nature brings the sun 2 warm
Also, it can bring gray skies 4 a storm
Believe in clocks 2 tell time
Listen 2 the bells chime
Believe in your heart and your mind
Believe in true love u can find
Do u believe it's 86,400 seconds in a day?
Believe we can chase the negativity away
U can believe u are a star
U can make it far
Put your mind into it
Don't quit
Keep believin'.

Interview I

The Announcer: *Welcome back 2 WFYM and with my special guest, Wohali Amayi. Welcome 2 the show, sir.*

Wohali Amayi: *Thank u so much 4 havin' me.*

The Announcer: *First, I want 2 congratulate u with the success of the first "Journey." That was a great collection of poems and I speak 4 everyone who has the first one that we all enjoyed every poem. How did u get started writing?*

Wohali: *Thank u. How I started was back in high school, we had 2 do a poem project where we had 2 come up with 10 characters including myself and present it in class. I didn't want 2 read mine, so I had someone read it 4 me. I got positive feedback from my classmates. From there, I just played around and started writing at home, kept them 2 myself.*

The Announcer: *That's great! How did u get into makin' the book?*

Wohali: *I was at work one day and I shared a couple 2 some co-workers and they all gave me great feedback. Some of them asked me did I have a book and I told them "No" and they were sayin' "U should make one." I never thought of makin' a book. From there, I took the poems I already had, then wrote more 2 make my first one. Later* *that year as Chauncey J. Lacey, "The Flow Of Poetry" was born. That was released in the Fall of 2020.*

The Announcer: *That was also a great collection as well, do u remember your first poem u wrote when u started?*

Wohali: *Yes, I do. It was included in "The Flow" the first poem was titled "The Art Of A Poet." Believe or not, that was written in 1999.*

The Announcer: *1999?! U held out that long?!*

Wohali: *(Laughing) Yes.*

The Announcer: *2 your co-workers, thank y'all! How did u feel after u released "The Flow?"*

Wohali: *Nervous!! I didn't know how the outcome was goin' 2 be. But after I got great feedback from all the fans, I felt great!*

The Announcer: *That's fantastic! Let's continue with some more poetry. Wohali Amayi, ladies and gentlemen!*

<u>Elements Of The Universe: Earth</u>

People of the Earth are grounded
Any Taurus, Virgo or Capricorn are focused
They are the ones who likes instruction
They are organized and show perfection
They have the wisdom 2 be a great leader
An earth person likes 2 keep things in order
People can find an earth person they can look up 2
They will show their love 2 u.

Elements Of The Universe: Air

The air symbol has the gift 4 teaching
People who are great communicators 2 be entertaining
They are creative thinkers
They could be great storytellers
A Gemini is not hard 2 find
Libras are brilliant in their own mind
Aquarius have an appetite 4 new information
Pair up with the air 2 have a love connection.

Elements Of The Universe: Water

Cancers, Pisces, Scorpios
U symbolize water that flows
U can be private and secretive
A deep level 2 be sensitive
Also, u can be deep creatively
U allow people 2 connect with others emotionally
Water has a rich imagination
A spiritual style that shows purification.

Elements Of The Universe: Fire

Fire people are dramatic
Energetic and enthusiastic
They are the party lovers
The passion 2 be the natural performers
The freedom 2 be impulsive
They love 2 be expressive
Aries, Leo, Sagittarius
Stay inspirational and humorous.

<u>Power In Numbers</u>

Everywhere u look, u can't help 2 stare
U see numbers everywhere
Everybody uses them all the time
Whether it's daytime or nighttime
It's in your mind so deep
Some people may count in their sleep
Numbers are powerful
Numbers are useful
Let's be exact
Let's add them, let's subtract
Multiply and divide
Keep your mind occupied
Let them fall in line
Start from 1 and end with 9.

Power In Numbers: One

We were all made from the originator
The one creator
U have the conscious personality
A daring spirit 2 express originality
U have the key 2 your own inspiration
U have the willpower and an urge of determination
A life lesson of takin' responsibility
U are confident
An inspiring person that's self-reliant.

<u>Power In Numbers: Two</u>

A person that's intuitive and adaptable
Who can balance bein' friendly and sociable
A nature of bein' romantic
Also courteous and diplomatic
Developing skills in communications
Learn 2 be a peacemaker in public relations
With plenty of cooperation and patience
You'll become a perfect balance.

<u>Power In Numbers: Three</u>

Emotional and expressive
Creative and sensitive
One who is entertaining
One who enjoys the freedom of loving
Expressing the joy of living
Good at speakin' your knowledge by communicating
Express yourself fully
Express yourself freely.

Power In Numbers: Four

U are the protector
U are the hardworker
U keep yourself in line
U are directly honest and have self-discipline
U can learn 2 be adaptable
But u can also be more flexible
U are commonly known as builders
4 enterprises as the founders.

<u>Power In Numbers: Five</u>

A person who's enthusiastic
One who can react quick
Broad-minded
Focused
The opportunity 2 travel 2 new places
Enjoy meeting new faces
Expect the unexpected of pleasant surprises.

<u>Power In Numbers: Six</u>

Emotional
Universal
Compassion
Vision
Good taste in style and beauty
A perfectionist in creativity.

<u>Power In Numbers: Seven</u>

Appreciate their honesty
They're trustworthy
Inspired in reading
Inspired in writing
Havin' a excellent memory
Learns through other personal experiences frequently.

Power In Numbers: Eight

A new beginning 2 be motivated
Determined
Desired 4 dominance
Leadership in dedication and perseverance
U aspire 2 a great accomplishment
A character of sound judgment.

Power In Numbers: Nine

Integrity
Sensitivity
Charismatic
Magnetic
An inner vision of wisdom and compassion
U can be idealistic with a great imagination.

<u>Natives Song</u>

Natives, get up
Natives, stand up
Come together, grab a hand
Form a band
Anoint each other with a smile
Let's move in style
Wave our hands in the air
Do it with flair
Stomp your feet
Feel the beat
Chant with me

Hei Ya, Hei Ya!
Hei Ya, Hei Ya!

Hear the drummers drummin'
This is our homecomin'
U know who u are
Everybody's shinin' like a star
This is our nation
This is our celebration
This is our land
Listen 2 our band
Chant with me

Hei Ya, Hei Ya!
Hei Ya, Hei Ya!

Human Computer

Everybody's lookin' into the future
The future could be filled with robots
Guess what?
We are robots
When we came into this world
We are programmed 2 function
Learned how 2 move in motion
Use your voice 4 communication
Use your body with emotion
Think about how your mind works
Check it out
Your daily routine
U may wake up at 6:15
Which leg u move first?
Which hand u brush your teeth?
Which foot u put a shoe in before the other?
Everybody is different from another
What time u walk out the door?
What day u go 2 the store?
We all have a mainframe
Capture all the info and knowledge 2 claim
We go through life upgrading ourselves
We pick up some viruses along the way
But we have 2 clean ourselves
Get rid of them, zap them away
Live long as we can
We're like robots, formed as human.

<u>How Long... (Part One)</u>

Time (tick tock)
Time (tick tock)

Second by second
Minute by minute
Hour by hour
How long is time?
Everything is fine
Can u measure time nonstop?
How long will it take 2 climb 2 the mountain top?
How many seconds 2 walk 2 the mailbox?
Count the time it'll take 2 put on socks

Time (tick tock)
Time (tick tock)

Run a mile
Hold a smile
The breath u hold
Thaw out from the cold
Drink a glass of H2O
How long the sun and the moon will glow?
The length of one commercial
A single informercial
How deep 2 dig a hole
Plant a flagpole

Time (tick tock)
Time (tick tock)

<u>How Long... (Part Two)</u>

Sing a song
A poem, how long?
Show an emotion
Swim in an ocean
A bird that flies through a town
A person's fever 2 drop down
The Earth turns
A fire that burns
A heart beats
Walk across the street
Stay in your lane
Fly overseas by plane
How long will u sleep?
How long will your mind think deep?
How long is fast 2 u?
How long is slow 4 u?
How much u have 2 give?
How long will u live?
Enjoy the time
Everything is fine
Times are different
Everything is a riddle
All answers will not be the same
Play the game
U can't cheat the time
Get yourself in line

Tick tock (time)
Tick tock (time)
Listen 2 the clock
Time (tick tock)
Time (tick tock)

Sunday's Alright 4 Football

Stadiums filled with roarin' fans
Coaches have their teams game plans
Referees and players hit the field
Give their quarterback a shield
One team using their defense
While the other use their offense
Touchdown they score as the crowd say
Rah, rah, rah, hey, hey, hey
Rah, rah, rah, hey, hey, hey
Sunday's alright 4 football
Give your friends a call
The day is ours
Give us a few hours
Break out the chips
Serve up some dips
Bring on the drinks and food
Watchin' the game with our eyes glued
'Til the team scores again, and we all say
Rah, rah, rah, hey, hey, hey
Rah, rah, rah, hey, hey, hey
Sunday's alright 4 football
Havin' ourselves a ball.

Reach Out, Come Together

Reach out, take my hand
Take a stand
Time 4 the world 2 come together
Time 2 love one another
Make each other smile again
Wake up people, time 2 work
No time 2 act like a jerk
Time 2 start a trend
Reach out, make a friend
We can make the world better
Either by phone or a letter
Make it happen today
Keep it goin' everyday
It'll do u no harm
Make someone feel special, make their heart warm
Reach out, take my hand
One by one, let's expand
Form a human chain
No more war, let's love and trust each other again.

Speakin' My Mind, Part One (Spoken Word)

A person walkin' down the street
Mindin' their own business
A person eatin' in a restaurant
Or maybe just waitin' on someone 2 meet
Just tryin' 2 have a good day
It's the one person that can spoil it
Or standin' in your way
Why is that?
That one person in your face pushin' your buttons
Until it turns into a conflict
I can be nice and ask u 2 leave me alone
The person wants 2 pick your bone
Everything is cool until u cross the line
The world goes into a decline
Don't call me a nigger
Cause I'm not
Don't call me a bitch
Cause I'm not
Don't call me a slave
Cause I'm not
Don't tell me 2 go back 2 Africa
Cause I didn't come from there
Respect me and I'll respect u
Stop bein' a disease like a flu.

Speakin' My Mind, Part Two (Spoken Word)

Lend a hand
Call me a friend
I'll answer u
Call me a brother
I'll answer u
U can call me partner
I'll answer u
Try me
Accept me as I am
I'm just like u
I'm just different
Don't be a bump in the road
Make it smoother
Quit separatin' the world with hate
Let's get along and come together
Keep the peace 4 each other
The world can be better.

The World's A Soap Opera

Ask the world "What's happenin'?"
The world is turnin'
U don't need a TV
Look around and see
It goes in the daytime
It goes in the nighttime
Everyday is a story
People tryin' 2 solve the mystery
The emotions of drama turned into rage
How did it get 2 this stage?
Families split into a rivalry
Danger stems from stupidity or jealousy
Where are the ones we can call a hero?
Bring the problems down 2 a zero
Where's the love?

Searchin' 4 Answers

Someday?
Will it happen one day?
Will we get there?
Questions asked, but no answers
Somebody tell me
Will we all be free?
Will the dream become real?
Can we seal the deal?
Why have so many attacks?
Why we put pressure on our backs?
Who's gonna take the weight?
Destroy the hate
What's goin' on, everybody's askin'
Everybody knows what's happenin'
Wake up
Get up
Stand up
Change up
Clean it up
Make up
U can make it better
Your life does matter
See it from my eyes
Clear the dark skies
Who's gonna save the world?
Who's gonna heal the world?
What's the world's resolution?
Who's got the solution?

<u>Stop The War</u>

What u fightin' 4?
Why start up a war?
What's it good 4?
The idea of causin' an uproar
What happened about talkin'?
Instead, u send your rockets flyin'
U set your bombs a-burstin'
Blowin' up buildings
Destroyin' family housings
Takin' the lives of the innocence
U feel good, don't u?
It's not necessary, it doesn't make sense
Stop the war, right now
Figure it out, u know how
U know u doin' wrong
Find a solution 2 get along
Find some peace
Tell the soldiers 2 cease fire
Stop makin' the death toll higher
Put your country at rest and ease
Stop the fight
Stop the war, right now.

*Dedicated 2 Ukraine

Where's The Future?

Lives shortly cut
Opportunity doors closed shut
Stray bullets flyin'
Young children dyin'
The world turnin' cold
What does the future hold?
Children are the future of today
Not if a negative act takes them away
What's goin' through their mind?
Why are u the corrupted kind?
The young will never be a sir or a madam
Because people like u don't give a damn
U didn't give a young one a chance 2 see
However, u still get 2 walk around free
U could've been the future's teacher
Teach the future of today 2 be a leader
Turn the world around from devastation
Make the world better 4 the next generation
I'm tired of sheddin' tears
I'm tired of livin' in fear
Where's the answer 2 "What's Going On?"
So many questions that can weigh a ton
Here's another one
Who's the future?

*Dedicated 2 the young ones lost from gun violence.

INTERMISSION

ALSO AVAILIBLE ON AMAZON.COM

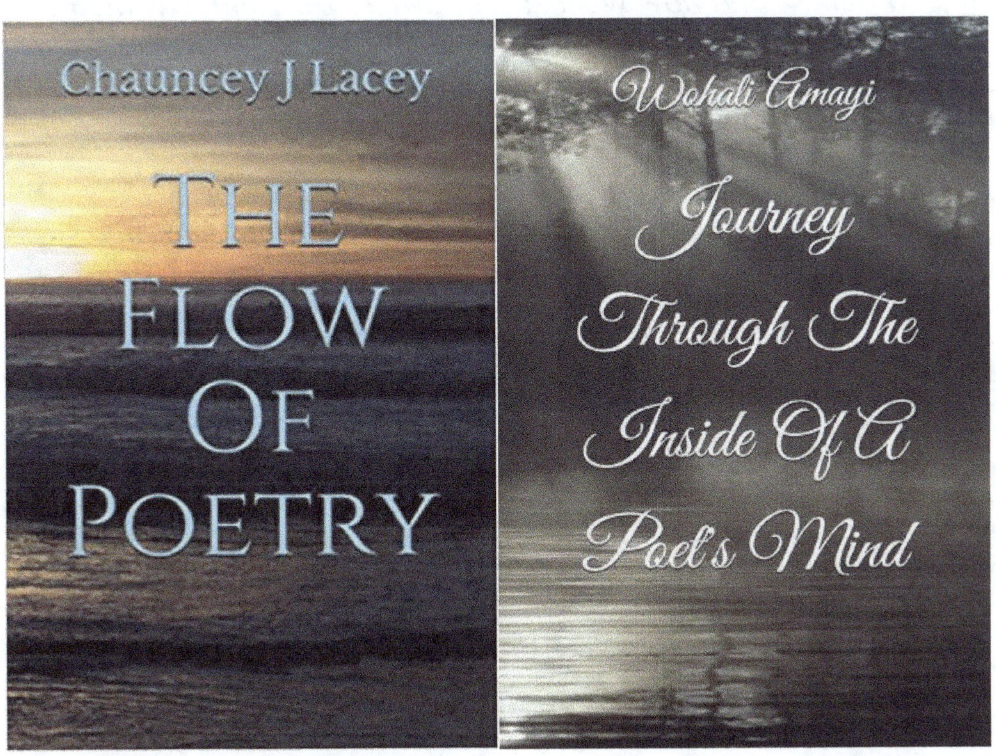

<table>
<tr><td>

Featured Poems:

Letter 2 U
The Art Of A Poet
The Soul Of Wind
Electric Soul
Freedom Song
...And many more!!

</td><td>

Featured Poems:

Free
Poem Of Romance
I Am
Spiritual Journey
Ice Cream Poetry
...And many more!!

</td></tr>
</table>

<h1 style="text-align:center"><u>Interview II</u></h1>

The Announcer: *Welcome back 2 the show with our special guest, Wohali Amayi. We were talkin' about his beginnings and the release of the first book "The Flow Of Poetry" and now we fast forward 2 2021 and saw the next release "Journey Through The Inside Of A Poet's Mind." How did this one come about?*

Wohali: *When "The Flow" was released in October 2020, people were askin' me was I goin' 2 do another one. I wasn't sure at the time if I was goin' 2 make another or not. While "The Flow" was still fresh then, I quietly started writing on New Years 2021, that was the beginning of what would become "Journey."*

The Announcer: *How did u come up with the title "Journey Through The Inside Of A Poet's Mind?"*

Wohali: *The title came after I was finishing the book, it didn't have a title until then. I had a few ideas then before I settled on "Journey." I felt that when people read the book, it would feel like I took them on a journey from my views. Kind of a visionary journey through words.*

The Announcer: *I think everyone here can agree all of your poems are great, how do u come up with the poems?*

Wohali: *Most of them come to me in my head, I'll try 2 write them down. Sometimes the poem can flow out and I'll complete the poem. Other times, I'll start on the poem and come back 2 finish them. 4 example, I had an idea of a poem that I started on and it took me a long time 2 finish, but I finally finished it.*

The Announcer: *Do u remember which poem it was?*

Wohali: *It was "Who Am I" from "The Flow Of Poetry." That one took me about 2 ½ years 2 finish. Every time I work on that one, I couldn't get it right or part of the poem I didn't like. That was the one poem that took me the longest time 2 write.*

The Announcer: *That is amazing! Wow! Let's get back 2 so more poetry!*

The Journey: The Return (Part One)

2020 started a flow of poetry
2021 took u on a journey
2 many situations happened, it was rough
Makes u want 2 scream "Enough!"
Will we get over the disease?
Will we ever get some peace?
Only time will tell
Send me an email
In the meantime, I'll give u a call
Look out your window, watch the snow fall
Grab some alphabet soup
Better yet, have some ice cream...2 scoops
Kick back and watch the circus on tv
Laugh with your funny bone, it's free
Enjoy the bells, whistles and buzzers
The world is spinnin' with colors
Flashback from today 2 the past
It's amazin' how the time flies fast.

<u>The Journey: The Return (Part Two)</u>

I find peace on an island
Enjoyin' myself with a drink, sittin' on the sand
Watchin' the sunset and the moonlight
The glow from above shinin' bright
It's only natural
The feelin' is spiritual
Cleanse my soul as I meditate
Deeply, my mind relaxes and create
I'm like a bird in the sky
I took u on a trip through the galaxy
A planet with an unknown name
The world was not the same
Value your life, give yourself a chance
Treat yourself 2 find love and romance
Make it a perfect day
I'll show my love with the perfect bouquet
Take me away from the darkness, find the light
I got 2 survive, I must finish the fight
The light is green, gotta go
I won't stop 'til my heart says so.

Poetic Jazz

Sittin' under a shaded tree
Readin' and writin' some poetry
Thinkin' of ideas in my head
Like layin' in my bed
Listenin' 2 the flow of jazz music
Combin' my hair with my afro pic
Improvisin' my vision with their sounds
Paintin' a picture in circled rounds
Takin' their smooth with the cool
As the words I develop from my tool
With their styles and class
Listen 2 Ella Fitzgerald shatter a champagne glass
Miles, Bird, Coltrane, Dizzy Gillespie
Duke, Thelonius Monk, Count Basie
"What A Wonderful World" says Satchmo
If u see Dolly, tell her "Hello"
Can't nobody scat like Cab Calloway
"Sassy" Sarah and Billie "Lady Day"
The fusion comes together as a soundtrack
Words and sounds blended perfect, tick 4 tack
They can be sweet from the soul
Only both of their rhythms are in control
Universal across the world, people can feel it
People can understand it
The relevance of them can stand the test of time
At any age and generation, it's just like fine wine.

Dance Battle

Challenge!
I'm callin' u out
U know what this is about
Find a spot
Show me what u got
Pump up the volume
Don't need a costume
Street clothes is all I need
Dance shoes indeed
I'll take u 2 Chicago, hit u with the 2-step
Switch it up 2 the runnin' man, give u some pep
Moonwalk like M.J. and glide
Get my crew and do the electric slide
Do a little boogie
Do a little woogie
The stage is hot
Who else want a shot?
Feel the beat thumpin'
Cha-cha one time, get the foot stompin'
Have one leg goin' crazy
With the other leg goin' stanky
I'm not done yet, I got some more
Drop down and do the worm on the floor
I'm break dancin'
On my head like a top spinnin'
Goin' old school like Rerun pop-lockin'
End the battle with the gangsta walkin'
It's over now
Tip your hat and take a bow.

Everybody come 2 the round table and vote
Who do u want 2 be the G.O.A.T.?
Who do u think is the best?
U can be the Greatest
Set the bar
In your own way, be a superstar
U can be the Baddest
The Bravest
The Grooviest
The Hippest
The Slickest
The Smoothest
The Funniest
The Tallest
The Fastest
The Quickest
The Smartest
The Coolest
The Toughest
Ladies, u can be the Sexiest
The Cutest
Put yourself 2 the test
Whatever your talent is, u can be the Best.

The Jungle

When u go 2 the jungle, beware
Look out 4 lions, tigers and bears
Don't do somethin' u may regret
Take a picture and make one upset
Run, run, run as fast as u can
Don't look 4 Tarzan
Save yourself and swing on a vine
Stay on the path in a straight line
Gotta make it 2 the sea
Watch out 4 that tree!
Swim boy swim!
Or be torn limb from limb
Made it out without a crumble
From the jungle rumble.

The Gunslinger

Howdy y'all!
In the Old West
A young cowboy, as great as the rest
Rollin' with a cloud of dust
One u can trust
Fast like lightning bolt
He strikes like an electric volt
When u call him, he'll be there in a dash
Takes care of his enemies and collects his cash
Ready and willin' 2 make his next notch
He takes a sip of scotch
When u yell "Draw"
BANG!! One in the jaw
A face u can't clone
His name is Blaze "Bullet" Stone
And his reliable source
"Flashin'" Whiskey is his horse
Never fear
Take care now partner, ya here!

Jive Talkin'

What's up Airhead?
Have u seen Knucklehead?
Next time u see him
Tell him 2 call Jim
He wants 2 meet up on Troll
Anyhoo, I got 2 take a stroll
I'm headin' 2 pick up a hambone
With oodles of noodles, that's awesome
What a humdinger
This is an ankle-biter
I know u heard about Kooky
He's in cahoots with Loopy
Yo Daddy-O!
Don't have a bellyache or the heave-ho
I told u not 2 buy the lemon from Marvy
Now u stuck with that jiffy
Well, I got 2 start my shift
I'm a fat cat on easy street
Get my drift.

The Looney Gang

Saturday mornings is a kid's caffeine
Watchin' bright colors across the tv screen
Listenin' 2 the sound effects
Lookin' at the flyin' objects
Elmer Fudd huntin' 4 the wabbit
I mean the rabbit (Bugs Bunny)
But somehow, Daffy takes the shot
If he's in disguise or not
I think Wile E. Coyote need 2 call the clerk
Ask them why the products don't work?
Tryin' 2 catch the Road Runner always backfire
He doesn't give up or retire
Tweety saw a "puddy tat"
Look out, here comes Sylvester the Cat
I say, I say I'll grab some popcorn
2 enjoy the southern rooster of Foghorn Leghorn
Other characters u can dig
French skunk Pepé Le Pew, The Martian, Porky Pig
One who's always spinnin'
The Tasmanian Devil, if u can understand what he's sayin'
Yosemite Sam, the outlaw gun-shootin'
Speedy Gonzales, the fastest mouse runnin'
All of them goofy and crazy
Can't get enough of them on any Saturday.

<u>A Haunted Night</u>

I dare u 2 ring the doorbell
Welcome 2 the Darkness Of Hell
Come in, come in
The opening of a blue coffin
Welcome, I'm Count Frederik
Want 2 see a trick?
Watch me as I put on my black hat
Lightning strikes, I turn into a bat
See me flyin'
The ghosts laughin'
A skeleton walkin'
The thick fog talkin'
The spirits are in your mind
You're runnin', no lights 2 find
The bells ring from the clock
All doors and windows are lock
Run, but u can't hide
No way 2 escape outside
The zombies comin' toward u
You're shakin' in fear and don't know what 2 do
U scream and yell
U run and fall into a dark well
A bright light flash
U wake up, wipe the sweat from your eyelash
A relief from a weird nightmare
That all started from a dare.

<u>Game Of Poker</u>

Got my stack of chips
Grab my cheese and salsa dips
Deal me some cards, placed my bet
Put on my poker face and I'm set
My first hand wasn't fair
I ended up with a pair
Deal me in
Got 2 turn this around and win
Got a better hand with a 3 of a kind
Raise the stakes, look out, 4 of a kind
Stack gettin' bigger
Give me a shot of liquor
Feelin' the rush
Can u beat my straight flush?
Goin' all in, focus on my face
10, Jack, Queen, King...Ace!!
The sound of the room goes hush
BAM!! Royal Flush!!
From the bottom 2 the top
I didn't stop
I claimed my fame
In this poker game.

The Road Of Life (Life's Journey)

Everyone has their own mind
The road of life is yours 2 find
The path u choose is up 2 u
Only u know what 2 do
U can travel short or long
The knowledge u gain can be strong
The road has twists and turns
Success is there 4 one who learns
Like travelin' on streets that are rough
People go through times when it's tough
People may run into a dead end
U can always reach out 2 a friend
Through ups and downs, we face challenges
Smooth them out with the necessary changes
Travel away from the storm
Life can be beautiful
It's your world, make it wonderful.

<u>Save Me</u>

Standin' out on the window ledge
I've been livin' on the edge
People lookin' up and see me
Screamin' "Don't jump!" at me
I close my eyes and I let go
The crowd gasps and yell "No!"
I should've thought twice, but it's 2 late
I chose my fate
Could this be the last dance?
Will I have a second chance?
As I'm fallin' down, I take my last breath
I come face 2 face 4 death
I close my eyes...
SPLASH!!
My life is saved from a devastating crash
I'm alive
I'll survive.

<u>I'm Alive</u>

I told u about a year ago
I won't stop until my heart says so
Well, it's true
I'm not through
I'm still here
Lend me your ear
I'm alive
As long as I'm talkin'
I'm alive
As long as I'm smilin'
I'm alive
I have a pair of legs made 4 standin'
I have a pair of feet made 4 walkin'
I'm alive
Blood in my veins flowin'
A smile that's glowin'
I'm alive
Feed me your love, feed me your energy
Great vibes comin' from me
If u shoot me down with negativity
I'll fire back with positivity
My body will allow me 2 keep livin'
I'm still standin'
Say it with me and say it loud
I'm alive, say it and be proud
I'M ALIVE!!

Interview III

The Announcer: _Welcome back everyone, I hope u are enjoyin' the show. We have Wohali Amayi here and "Journey 2." How did this one start out?_

Wohali: _As most people know, last October, I lost my Mom. She…(sigh, pause)_

The Announcer: _Take your time, brother._

Wohali: _…she passed away 2 days after "Journey" was released. We got a chance to celebrate the release together. I know that she is smilin' down, she's still here. That was a tough time 4 me and my family. I thought about not writing anymore, until a friend of mine talked me into doin' another book and dedicating it 2 her. I was still undecided at the time whether if I wanted 2 or had the strength 2 do that. The beginning of "Journey 2" started with a poem that would become a gift 2 my sister and her husband. Me, my Dad, my nephew and my brother had a get together with him and after the outing, he asked me about writing a poem 4 them and I accepted. My sister didn't know about it all, so it became a surprise 2 her. I presented the poem 2 them at their wedding and that's how this one started, "Journey 2." And I also want 2 thank my friend who gave me a push 2 make this happen._

The Announcer: _We want 2 thank u 4 this collection. In my opinion, from reading this one, I believe u have_ *another fantastic book on your hands. We want 2 congratulate u on your success and hope 2 see more in the future. Thank u 4 comin' on the show 2 share with our audience. Ladies and gentlemen, let's have a round of applause 4 Wohali Amayi!*

Wohali: *Thank u 4 havin' me, I appreciate it.*

Dear Friend/Brother

It's not fair
It's not easy 2 see an empty chair
Without u here
It's not fair
It's hard 2 say goodbye
Without seein' u eye 2 eye
YaHaWah called u home today
Let him take the pain and suffering away
As a tear falls from the eye
There's another angel in the sky
We all know that we'll miss u my friend
Or some of us will say my brother
A friendship that'll never end
There'll never be another
One day we'll reunite
When the time is right.

*Dedicated 2 Toney Bridges

A Mother's Love

U bring bundles of joy 2 the world
Life forms of a boy or a girl
With the love u give wrapped in your arms
U give us wisdom and special charms
U spoil us all with your warmth
From the beginning of our birth
U feed the nutrients 2 make our bodies grow
And help give us the knowledge 2 fill the inner soul
U put clothes on our backs
U keep our minds on the right tracks
U are there 2 clean our wounds when we fall
A smile on your face when u hear our call
Your children can start their family tree
Your love and spirit is planted in me
Every day, every year
Thank u 4 the life I have here.

*Previously Released

<u>Diamond</u>

On a beautiful day in May of 1957
A beautiful gift from Heaven
From the parents of Beasley & Maggie
U are the baby of the family
Who would've thought 1974 will be great
4 u, u met your soulmate
Years later, got married and started a family
Brought 2 children 4 the world 2 see
When u was called 2 come home, it was a huge blow
I was at my all-time low
Torn 2 pieces, missin' the smile on your face
Everything u did, no one can take your place
Right now, as I'm wishin' u was here
I can't help myself sheddin' a tear
Deep down inside, in spirit, u are still here
I never said goodbye, because u are still here
I look at my dad and sister, u are still here
I look at your sisters, u are still here
I see u
I miss u
I look up 2 the night skies
I watch 4 the twinklin' stars of your eyes.

*4 my Mom

Peaceful Trail

I'm walkin' in nature
Feelin' the crisp air so pure
My mind calms and clears
Gentle winds whispers in my ears
Watchin' the leaves sway in different directions
All the trees shaped with perfection
The right amount of shade
Coolin' my body as the negativity fade
Hearin' the birds sing in harmony
I'm struttin' slow and steady
The trail leads me 2 a beautiful waterfall
This path is the right call
The mist kisses my face
I'm in the perfect place
Watchin' the waves travel down the stream
I lay down and daydream
My own peaceful getaway
2 live here everyday.

<u>Island Tropics</u>

My boat movin' with the motion
Cruisin' with the waves of the ocean
I find myself at a tropical island
Walkin' on the warm sand
A beautiful scenery, full of palm trees
The warmth of the air wavin' the green leaves
Hearin' the birds singin'
Listenin' 2 the parrots talkin'
A quiet resort 2 go swimmin'
Perfect 4 fishin'
A place 2 enjoy the sunshine
Gatherin' fresh fruits from the vine
Deep in the forest, I find a hut
Surrounded with orchids and trees filled with coconuts
Lookin' out the scenery, watchin' the moonlight
Glowin' bright, such a beautiful sight.

Caribbean Tour

I'm packin' my bags 4 a vacation
A Caribbean getaway invasion
Hit the beaches, chill under a palm tree
Let myself go and be free
A place 4 relaxation
Explore their cultural traditions
Watch me zip-line in St. Lucia
Sip me a tropical Bahama mama
Play some slots at the casinos
Dance 2 the calypso music in Barbados
I'm lovin' it here in Cuba
Gotta take a cruise 2 Jamaica and Aruba
Take me a flight 2 Puerto Rico
Enjoy the cuisines in Trinidad & Tobago
My home away from home
An adventure of the island syndrome.

Pulse Pattern

I vision u like the sound of music
Your stroll is rhythmic
U walk in an orchestrated matter
Makes my heart pitter-patter
Your hips move left 2 right
Movin' in rhythm day and night
It's like a drum beat
I pat my feet
With the beat of my heart
Our rhythms can be a work of art
Somethin' pure and affectionate
It'll be forever relevant
Let's compose a love song
A tune so strong
Made 4 everlastin' and lifelong.

<u>Melanated Coffee</u>

I need a morning pick me up
Lookin' around 4 my cup
Make my day better
Enjoy the pleasant weather
I need a cup of coffee
Smooth and creamy
Just the way I like it
Give me the right hit
She's just right 4 me
A beautiful one I love 2 see
Melanated skin, so silky and sweet
From her head down 2 her feet
Doesn't matter if she's mocha
She can be my hot cocoa
Creamy, rich and dark
Send me the right spark
Strong and rich from the heart
She's truly a gift from a work of art.

<u>Honey</u>

Outside my window
I vision an hourglass shadow
Look at your beautiful curves
Heart beatin' fast, calm down my nerves
My head starts 2 spin
Smooth golden brown skin
Kisses sweet like honey
Love so thick and sticky
Your soft, sweet voice melts my soul
Your love is in control
U glowin' like a neon
Your touch turns me on
You're standin' there like a tasty treat
Let me be the one 2 sweep u off your feet.

Beautiful Lady

Beautiful lady u are
Your eyes twinkle like a star
Your hair flowin' in the air
U make me stop and stare
With your kissable lips
I love 2 grip your hips
Listenin' 2 your sweet talk
Watchin' the rhythm of your walk
Your smile light up like the sunshine that glows
I rest my head on your soft pillows
From head 2 toe, u are beautiful
Fill me up with your love till I'm full
Your mind is beautiful
Your body is beautiful
Your soul is beautiful
Your style is beautiful
Your touch is beautiful
U know u are beautiful
Never mind what people say
Lady, u are beautiful.

The Energy Of Love

Enter in the kingdom of love
Don't be afraid love
Tonight will be a winner
Spend it with a candlelight dinner
A glass of champagne
Your presence I'll entertain
Soft music 2 slow dance
Feel each other's romance
Let our love flow through our bodies spiritually
Feelin' each other mentally
Our eyes connect instantly
Our hearts beat in rhythm constantly
My hands glidin' on your curves
The electricity excites my nerves
The love connection begins 2 heat
As our kisses meet
Give me a one-way ticket without an intermission
I'm full of non-stop love's ambition
Open up your love darling
Let me come in and make it everlasting
Gazin' into your eyes
As our love temperature rises
Our fire of love burns
Our world of love turns
Let yourself go
Let your love flow
We're driftin' away into paradise
All night until the morning sunrise.

<u>Together</u>

One meets another
They introduce each other
Look into each other's eyes
Vibes flowin' like butterflies
Cupid paired 2 hearts
With his arrow shaped darts
Love begins goin' out on dates
Love turns them into soulmates
One gets down on bended knee
One asks "Will u marry me?"
"Yes!" is the answer!
Do u agree?
2 begin a new as Husband & Wife
A new chapter in life
Love each other
Trust each other
Listen 2 each other
Compromise with one another
Forever in love, u can't go wrong
2 hearts will be everlasting and lifelong.

<u>Soulmate (Love)</u>

See me
Watch me
Talk 2 me
Listen 2 me
Hear me

Love me

Smile with me
Joke with me
Laugh with me
Cry with me
Comfort me
Lean on me

Love me

Hold me
Feel me
Hug me
Caress me
Kiss me
Make love with me

Love me

Stand by me
Sit with me
Chill with me
Think with me
Meditate with me
Be there with me
Trust me

Love me 4 who I am
I'll love u 4 who u are.

Daytime/A Dreamer's Dream

Early morning, the sun's risin'
The view is amazin'
Gotta get up and get myself together
I'm the human computer
Fix me some breakfast
Mix in some spices, quick fast
Put them in a dish
Take in a bite, delish
Need 2 make a round
I need 2 feel the touch of Earth's ground
Feel the energy from the sun, I daydream
I vision I was on an island with a water stream
With a beautiful, melanated coffee-skinned lady
I couldn't believe it, her name is Honey
Holdin' hands, walkin' on a trail that's peaceful
I found my soulmate, I'm thankful
Our love is priceless
I won't hide my feelings I express
The whispers of the wind playin' our song
A universal rhapsody tune we can dance along
With a smile on my face
And with u by my side, I love this place
As the sun begins 2 set
This dream is one I'll never forget.

Raindrop Rhapsody

Raindrops, sing your song
Whether it's short or long
Sing a few lullabies
As I close my eyes
My soul will soothe
As the rain whispers so smooth
Rain rain rain
Sing away my pain
Chase my blues away
Send my dreams today
I'm meditating
Keep singing
I'm smilin'
I'm relaxin'.

Sunset

A warm Thursday evening
Sittin' outside relaxin'
It's after 7
2 be exact, 7:11
I sip my drink
Ideas flowin' in my mind as I think
I watch the sun travels down 2 set
The orange glow in the sky, I bet
Reflections in the water shinin'
Energy from the waves is a beautiful feelin'
A glorious picture
From the works of Mother Nature
Like a painting, a perfect 10
I love 2 watch it over and over again.

Whispers Of The Wind

The breeze feels so good
U put my soul in a relaxed mood
The gentle flow talks 2 me
This is the right place 2 be
U cool me down when I'm hot
U warm me with a gentle shot
The signal of a storm headin' my way
I feel your touch when u push me away
When the moon comes out at night
U comfort me with love that's just right.

<u>Dreams</u>

Now I lay down 2 sleep
My mind is restin' deep
My body is in the zone
Into a dream world of my own
Everybody's dreams are different
It could be from the past or current
Dream about livin' in a different time frame
Dream about bein' in a video game
Reach out 2 touch a twinklin' star
Dream 2 fly in the sky with a car
Dream about the world without a gun
Dream about a loved one
A dream that's priceless 2 me
Somehow, someday... a dream can become a reality.

The Announcer: *We hope u enjoyed the show. We thank our special guest, Wohali Amayi 4 sharin' his new collection. This is WFYM, I'm The Announcer sayin' "Peace & Shalom" 2 all!*

Remembering the memory of:

Mary Flucker

Toney Bridges

George Barbee

I dedicate this book 2 my mother,
Aliheligi Tsisqua El
(05/28/1957-10/05/21)

*All poems written from November 2021-July 2022, except "A Mother's Love" (from "Journey Through The Inside Of A Poet's Mind)

<u>Wohali's Wa'Do's (Thank U's)</u>

Wa'Do 2 YaHaWah

Wa'Do 2 my family, my extended family, my friends 4 all of your love and support. Much love 2 all of u!

Contact: blueemerald9@protonmail.com

Feel free 2 leave your reviews/feedback also on Amazon.com